MW00595413

Famous & Fun Deluxe Collection

26 Pieces from Famous & Fun:
Pop, Classics, Favorites, Rock, Duets

Carol Matz

Famous & Fun Deluxe Collection, Book 1, contains 26 well-loved selections drawn from the following books:

- Famous & Fun Pop, Book 1
- Famous & Fun Favorites, Book 1
- Famous & Fun Duets, Book 1
- Famous & Fun Classics, Book 1
- Famous & Fun Rock, Book 1
- Famous & Fun Pop Duets, Book 1

These teacher-tested arrangements are student favorites, and can be used as a supplement to any method. No eighth notes or dotted-quarter rhythms are used. In addition to the wide variety of styles featured in this collection, several equal-part (primo/secondo) duets are also included for students to have fun with ensemble playing.

Carol Matz

Alfred

Produced by
Alfred Music
P.O. Box 10003
Van Nuys, CA 91410-0003
alfred.com

Printed in USA.

ISBN-10: 0-7390-9866-7
ISBN-13: 978-0-7390-9866-0

Supercalifragilisticexpialidocious

(from Walt Disney's "Mary Poppins")

Words and Music by
Richard M. Sherman and Robert B. Sherman
Arranged by Carol Matz

Brightly

Su - per - cal - i - frag - il - is - tic - ex - pi - al - i - do - cious!

E - ven though the sound of it is some-thing quite a - tro - cious,

DUET PART (Student plays one octave higher)

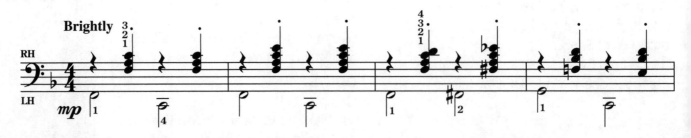

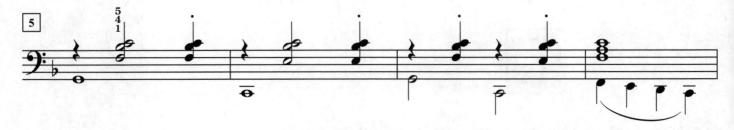

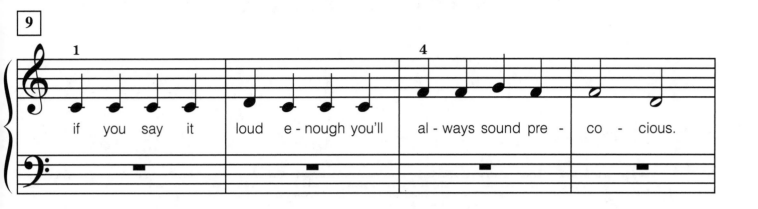

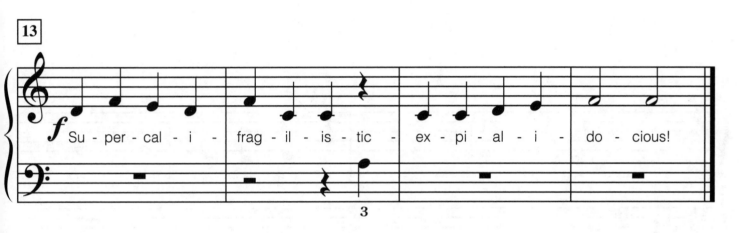

DUET PART (Continued)

This Land Is Your Land

Words and Music by Woody Guthrie
Arranged by Carol Matz

Cheerfully

This land is your land, this land is my land,

from Cal - i - for - nia to the New York is - land,

DUET PART (Student plays one octave higher)

Cheerfully

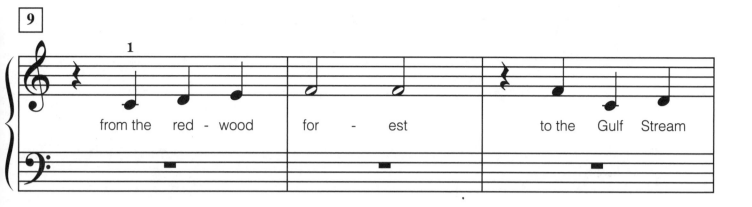

from the red - wood for - est to the Gulf Stream

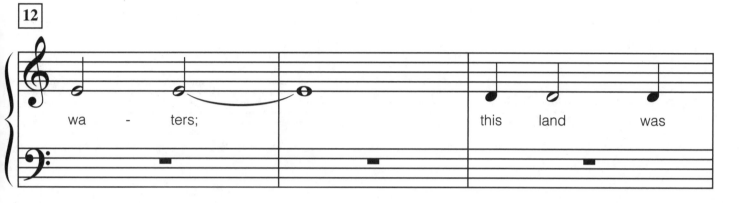

wa - ters; this land was

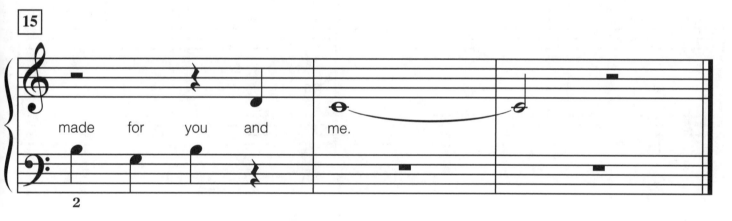

made for you and me.

DUET PART (Continued)

Scooby Doo, Where Are You?

Words and Music by
David Mook and Ben Raleigh
Arranged by Carol Matz

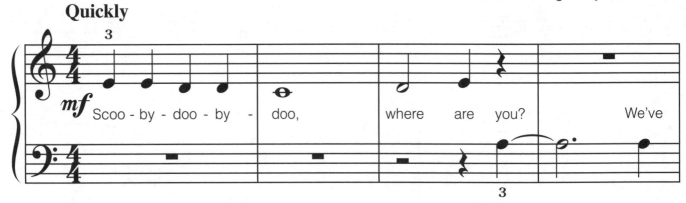

Scoo - by - doo - by - doo, where are you? We've

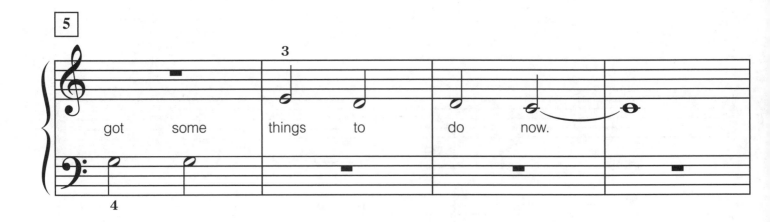

got some things to do now.

DUET PART (Student plays one octave higher)

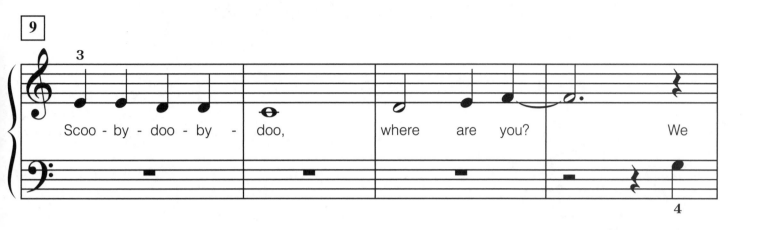

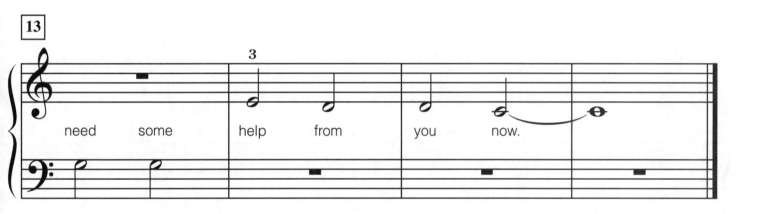

DUET PART (Continued)

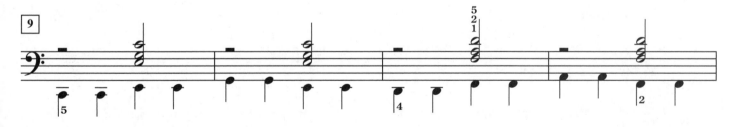

Over the Rainbow

(from the M-G-M Motion Picture "The Wizard of Oz")

Music by Harold Arlen
Lyric by E. Y. Harburg
Arranged by Carol Matz

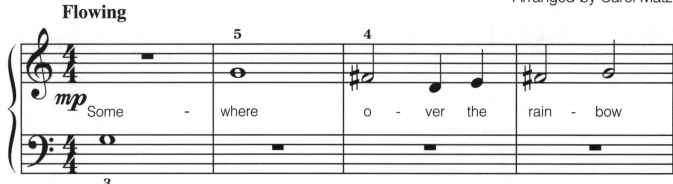

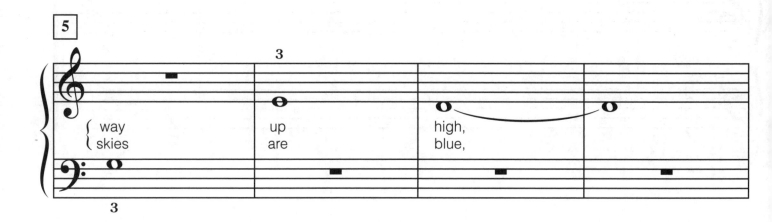

DUET PART (Student plays one octave higher)

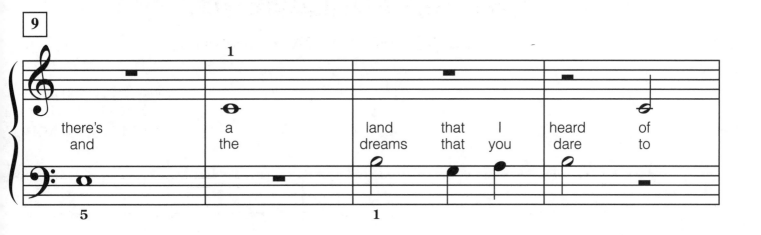

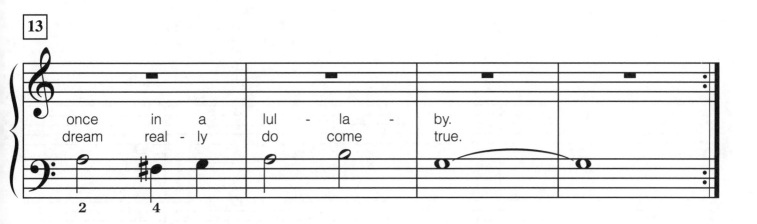

DUET PART (Continued)

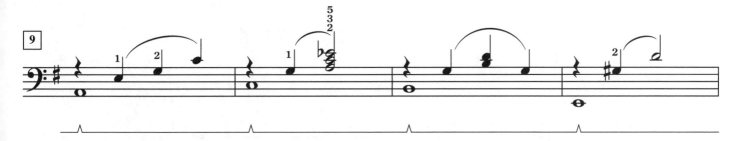

Can You Feel the Love Tonight

(from Walt Disney's "The Lion King")

Music by Elton John
Words by Tim Rice
Arranged by Carol Matz

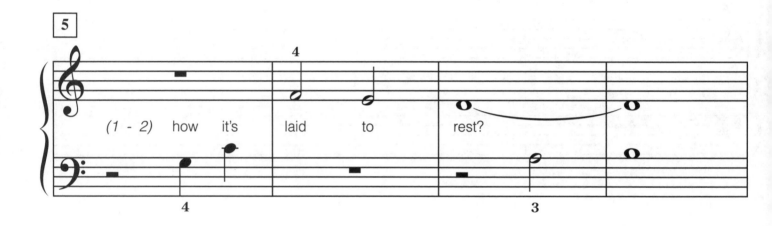

DUET PART (Student plays one octave higher)

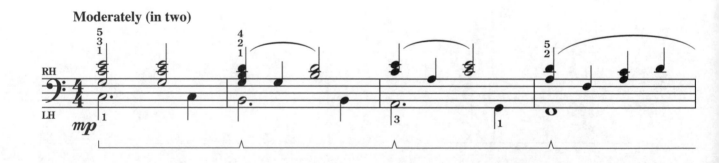

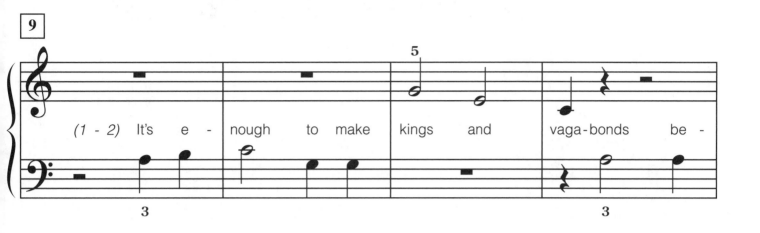

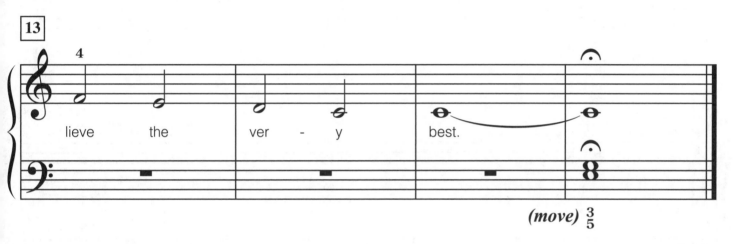

DUET PART (Continued)

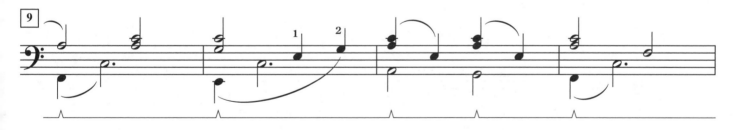

On Wings of Song

Felix Mendelssohn (1809–1847)
Arranged by Carol Matz

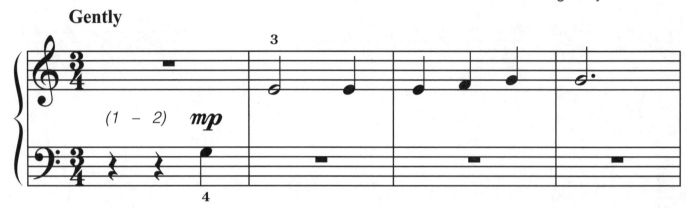

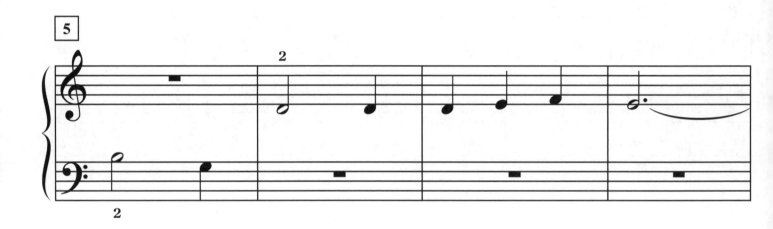

DUET PART (Student plays one octave higher)

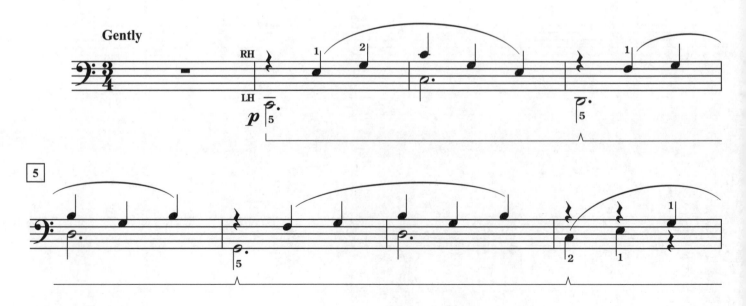

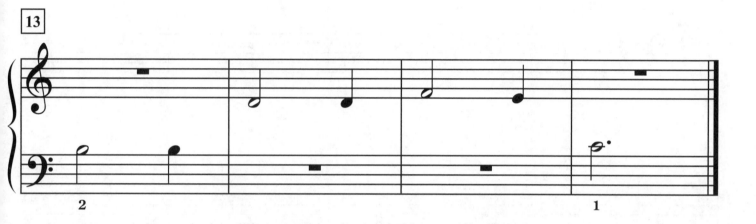

DUET PART (Continued)

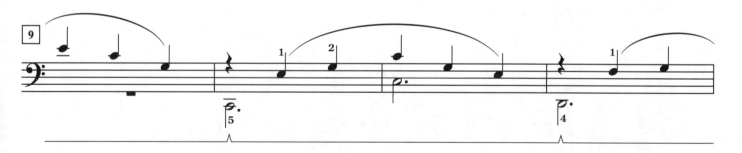

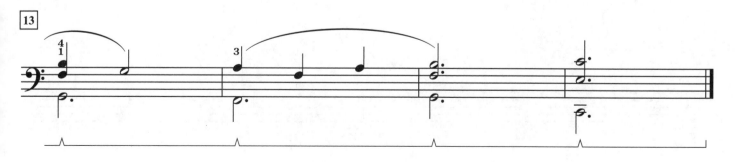

Barcarolle

(from the opera *The Tales of Hoffman*)

Jacques Offenbach (1819–1880)
Arranged by Carol Matz

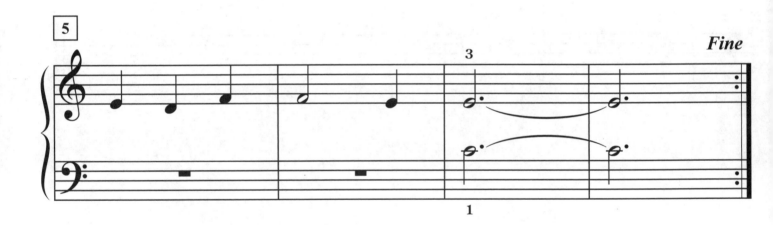

DUET PART (Student plays one octave higher)

(Go back to the beginning and play to Fine)

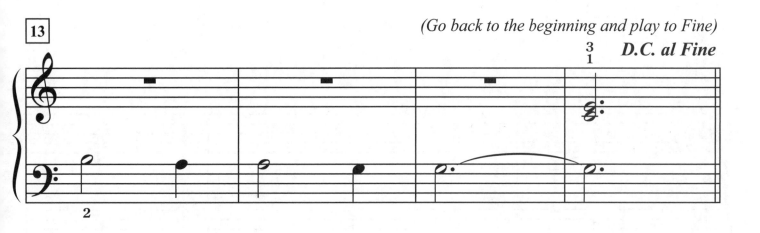

DUET PART (Continued)

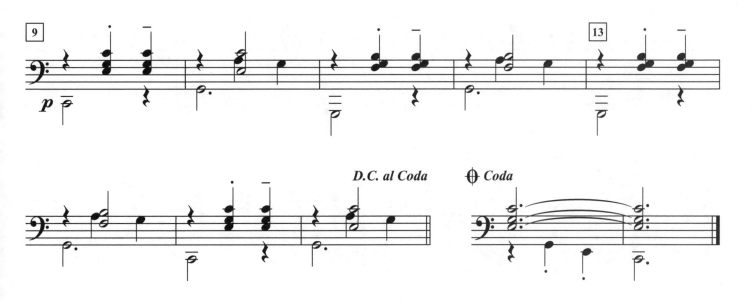

Theme from
Swan Lake

Peter Ilyich Tchaikovsky (1840–1893)
Arranged by Carol Matz

Moderately

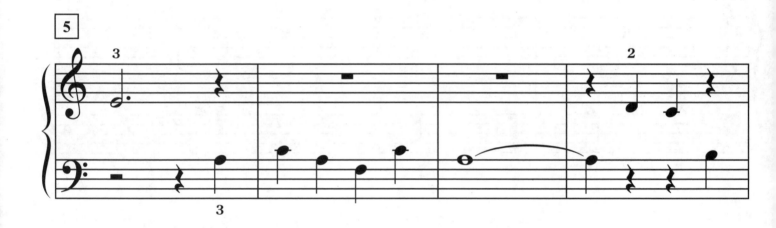

DUET PART (Student plays one octave higher)

Moderately

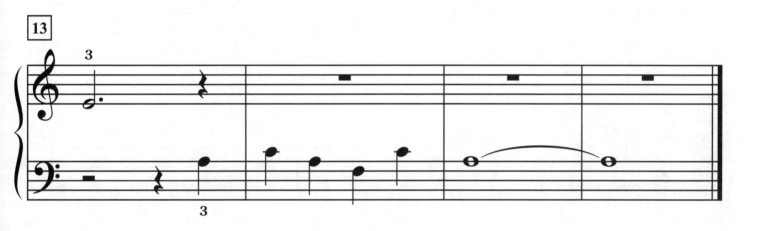

DUET PART (Continued)

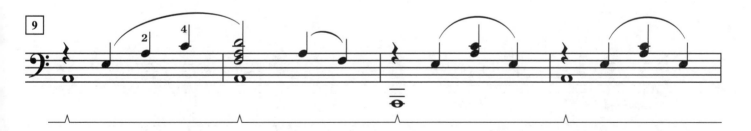

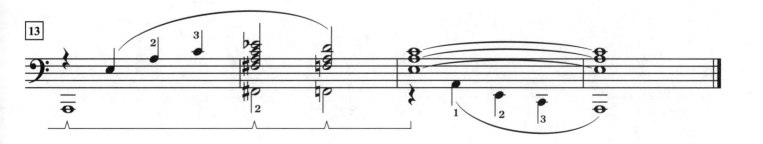

Theme from
Trumpet Concerto in E-flat

Franz Joseph Haydn (1732–1809)
Arranged by Carol Matz

Cheerfully

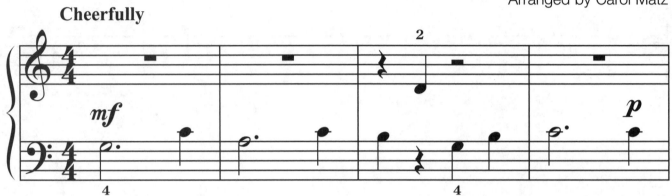

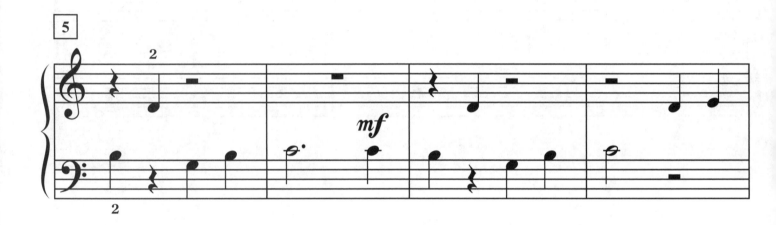

DUET PART (Student plays one octave higher)

Cheerfully

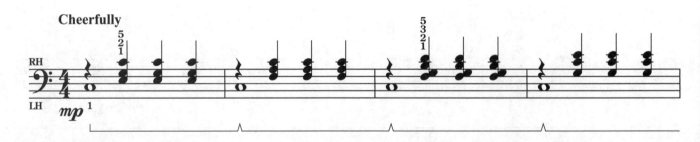

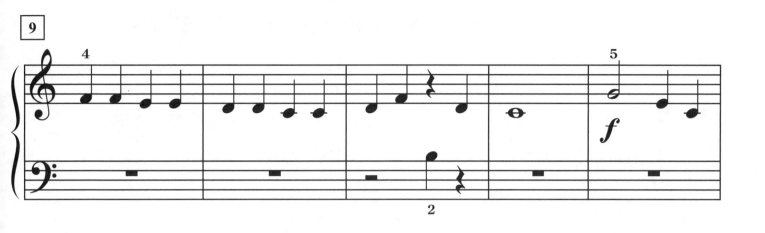

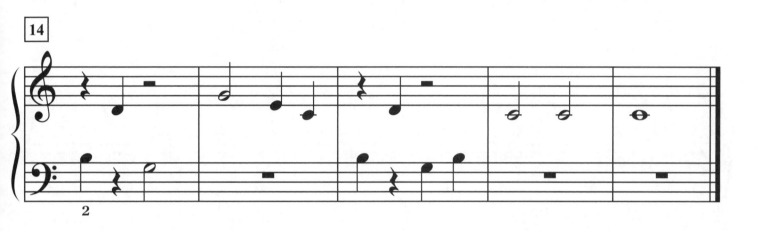

DUET PART (Continued)

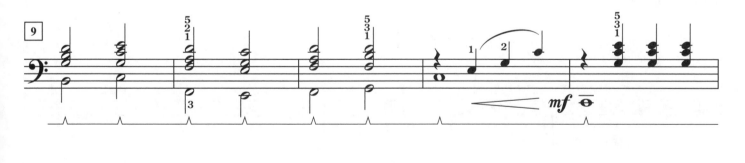

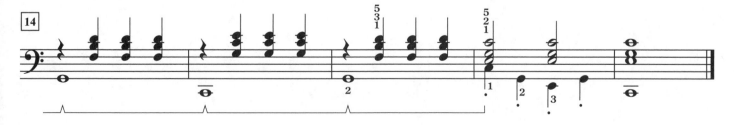

Eine Kleine Nachtmusik

("A Little Night Music," First Movement)

Wolfgang Amadeus Mozart (1756–1791)
Arranged by Carol Matz

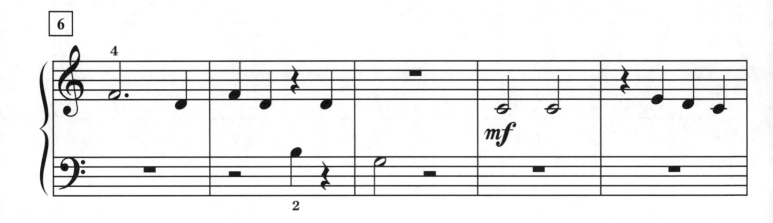

DUET PART (Student plays one octave higher)

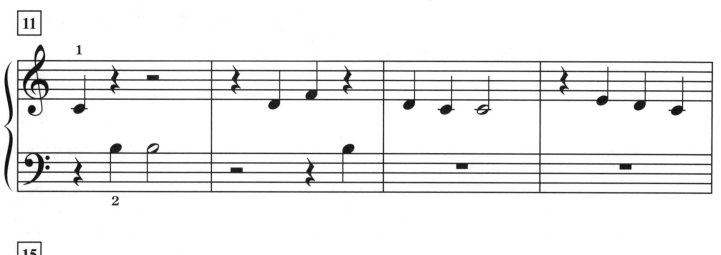

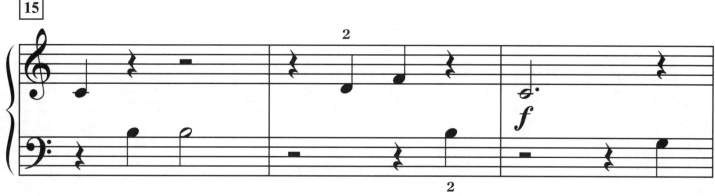

DUET PART (Continued)

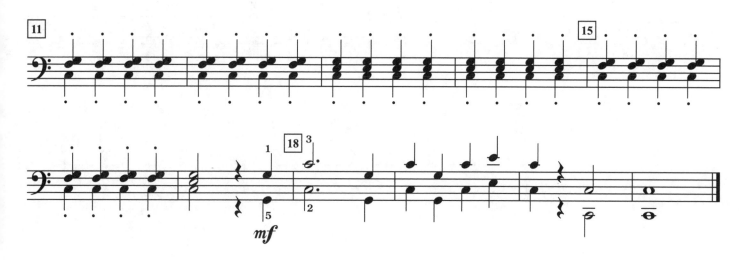

Overture to
The Barber of Seville

Gioachino Rossini (1792–1868)
Arranged by Carol Matz

DUET PART

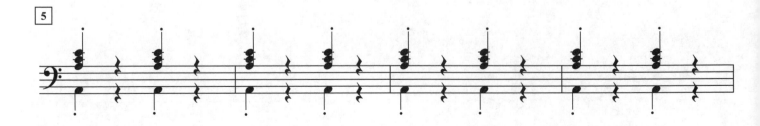

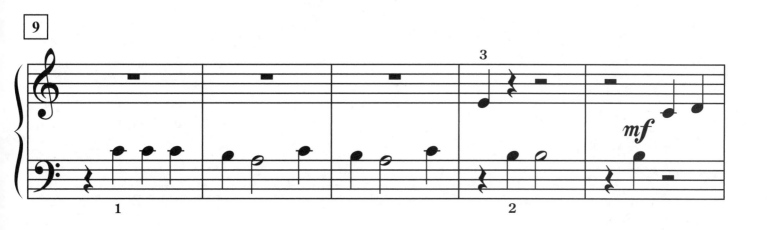

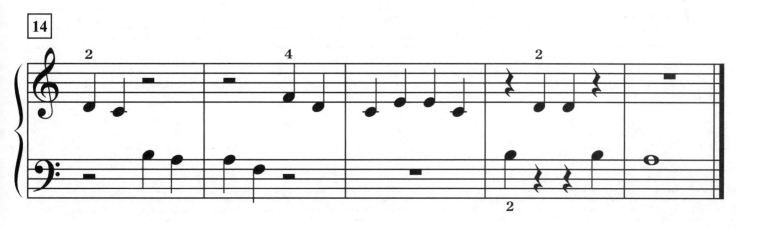

DUET PART (Continued)

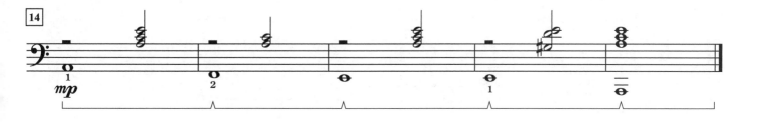

23

This Old Man

Traditional
Arranged by Carol Matz

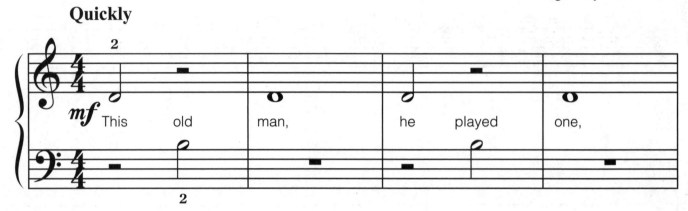

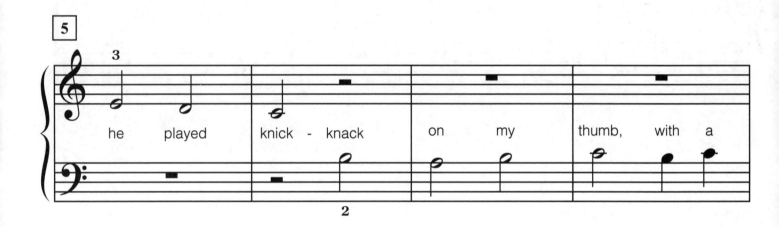

DUET PART (Student plays one octave higher)

knick - knack,   pad - dy whack,   give a dog a   bone,

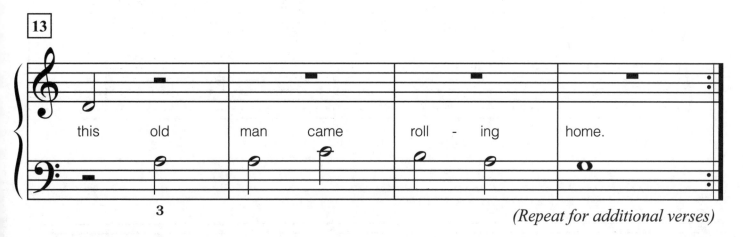

this   old   man came   roll - ing   home.

(Repeat for additional verses)

2. This old man, he played two,
   he played knick-knack on my shoe....

3. ... three ... on my knee....

4. ... four ... on my door....

5. ... five ... on my hive....

6. ... six ... on my sticks....

7. ... seven ... up to heaven....

8. ... eight ... on my gate....

9. ... nine ... on my vine....

10. ... ten ... once again....

DUET PART (Continued)

(Repeat for additional verses)

The Wheels on the Bus

Traditional
Arranged by Carol Matz

Quickly

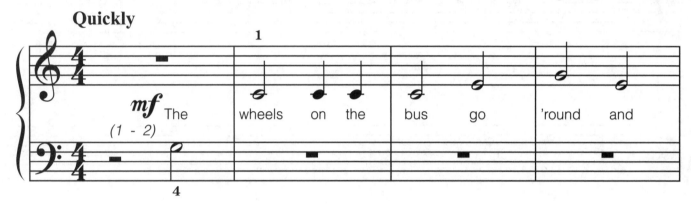

The wheels on the bus go 'round and

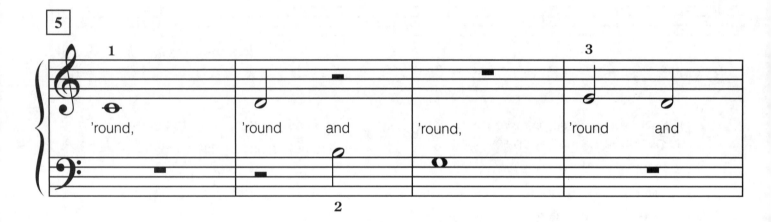

'round, 'round and 'round, 'round and

DUET PART (Student plays one octave higher)

Quickly, in two

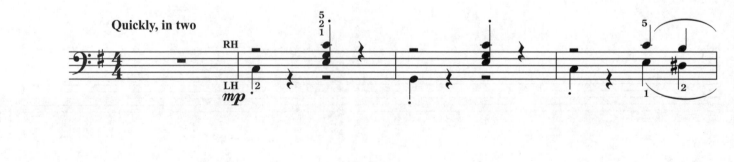

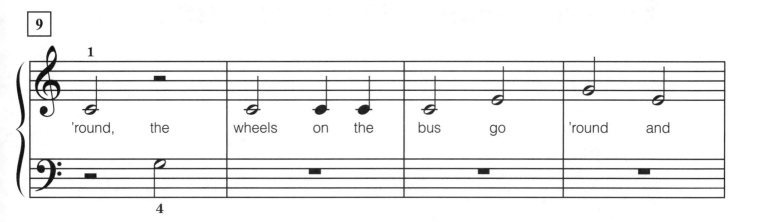

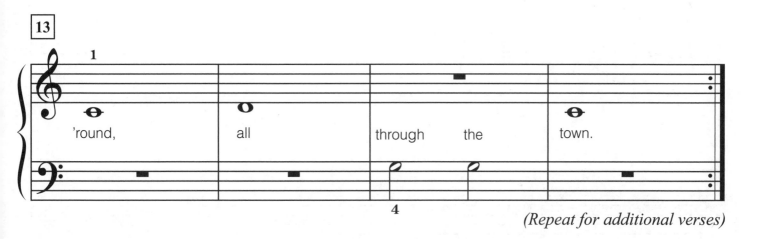

(Repeat for additional verses)

2. The wipers on the bus go "swish, swish, swish,"....
3. The people on the bus go up and down,....
4. The horn on the bus goes "beep, beep, beep,"....

DUET PART (Continued)

(Repeat for additional verses)

The Bear Went Over the Mountain

Traditional
Arranged by Carol Matz

Smoothly

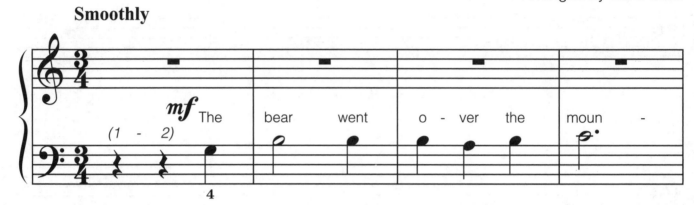

5

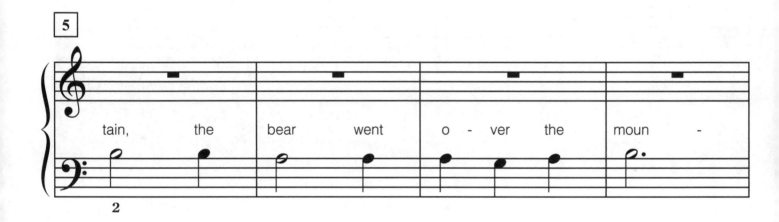

DUET PART (Student plays one octave higher)

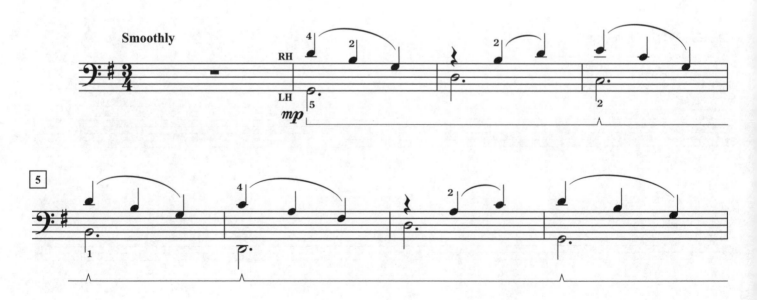

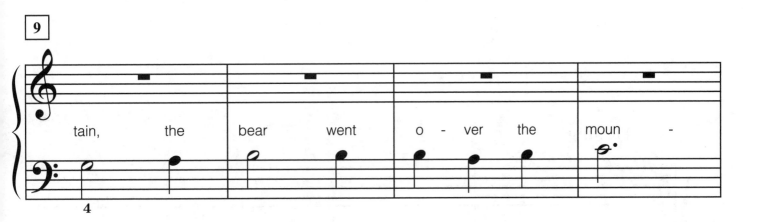

DUET PART (Continued)

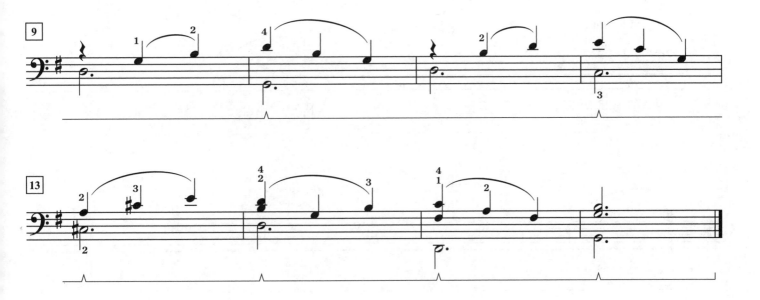

Row, Row, Row Your Boat

Traditional
Arranged by Carol Matz

Flowing

Row,   row,   row   your   boat

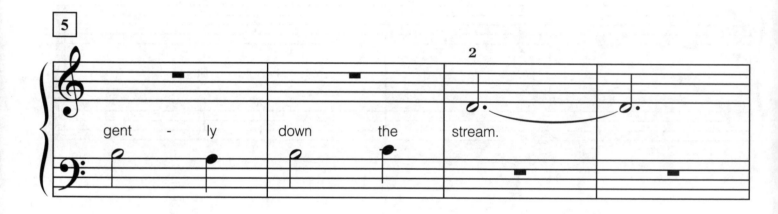

gent - ly   down   the   stream.

DUET PART (Student plays one octave higher)

Flowing

cresc.

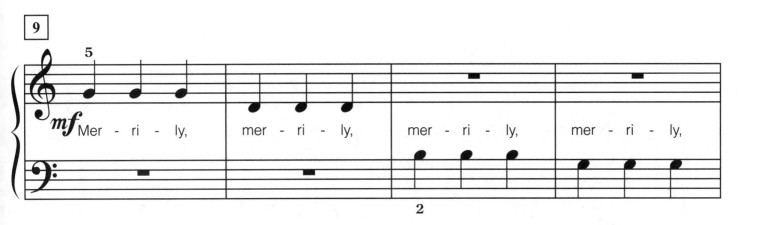

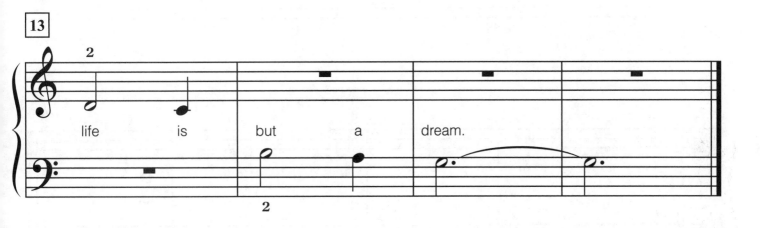

DUET PART (Continued)

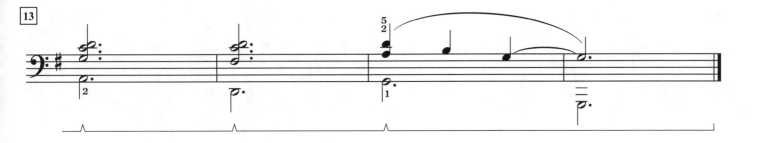

Alouette

Traditional
Arranged by Carol Matz

DUET PART (Student plays one octave higher)

(Go back to the beginning and play to Fine)
D.C. al Fine

DUET PART (Continued)

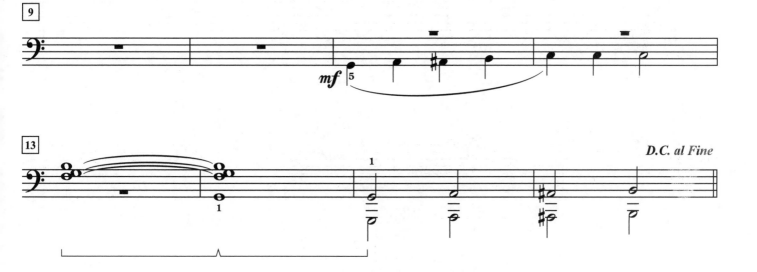

Bye Bye Love

Words and Music by
Boudleaux Bryant and Felice Bryant
Arranged by Carol Matz

Moderately

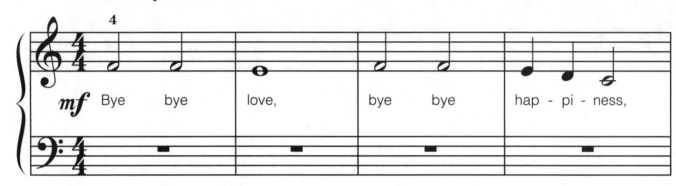

Bye bye love, bye bye hap - pi - ness,

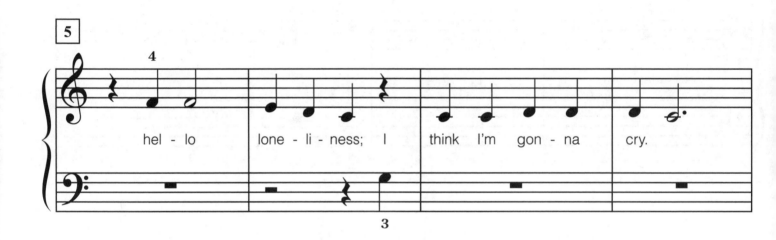

hel - lo lone - li - ness; I think I'm gon - na cry.

DUET PART (Student plays one octave higher)

Moderately

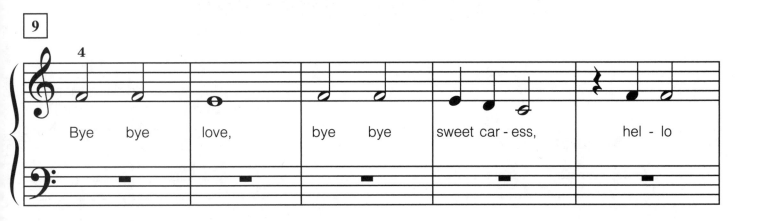

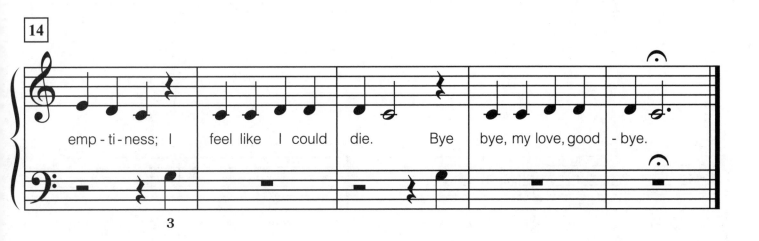

DUET PART (Continued)

Stairway to Heaven

Words and Music by
Jimmy Page and Robert Plant
Arranged by Carol Matz

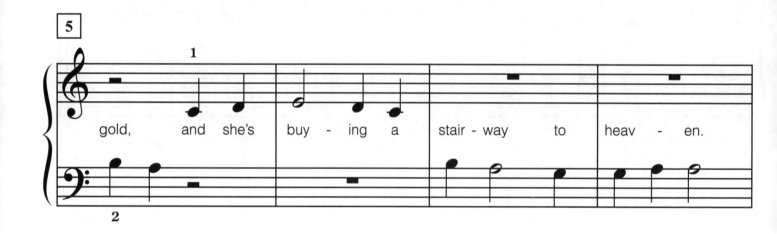

DUET PART (Student plays one octave higher)

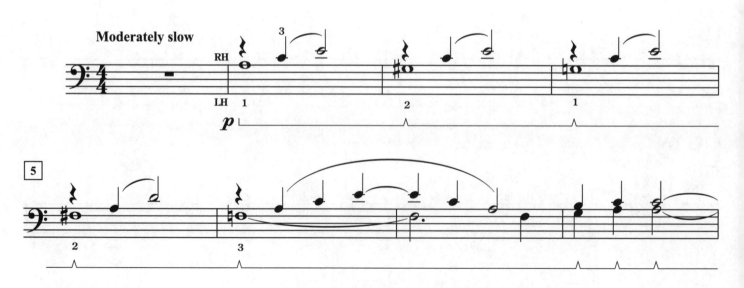

DUET PART (Continued)

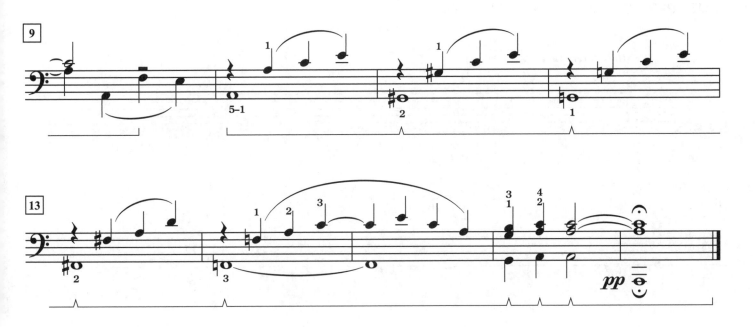

(We're Gonna)
Rock Around the Clock

Words and Music by
Max C. Freedman and Jimmy De Knight
Arranged by Carol Matz

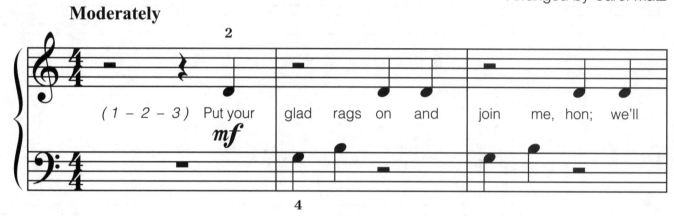

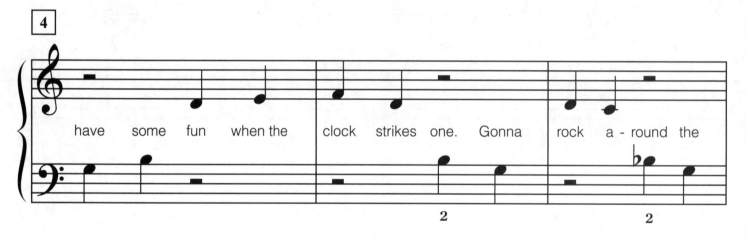

DUET PART (Student plays one octave higher)

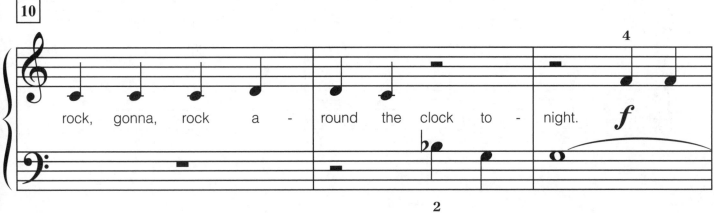

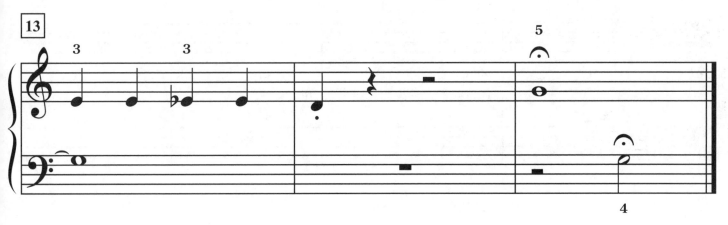

DUET PART (Continued)

The Lion Sleeps Tonight

New Lyric and Revised Music by
George David Weiss, Hugo Peretti
and Luigi Creatore
Arranged by Carol Matz

In the jun - gle, the might - y jun - gle, the

li - on sleeps to - night.

DUET PART (Student plays one octave higher)

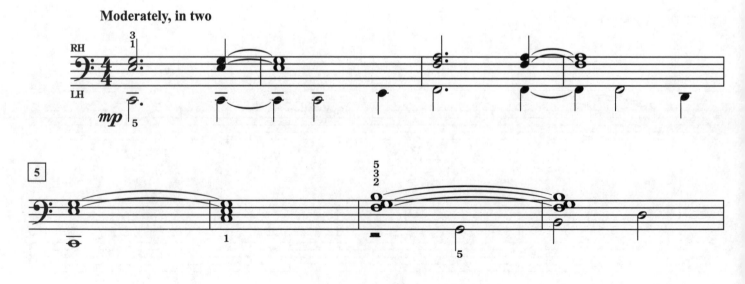

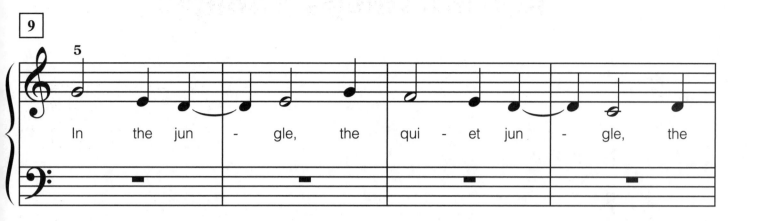

In the jun - gle, the qui - et jun - gle, the

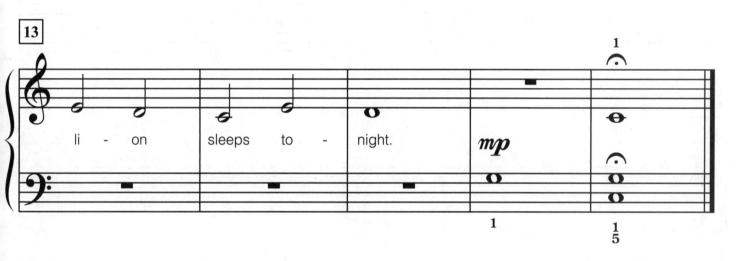

li - on sleeps to - night.

mp

DUET PART (Continued)

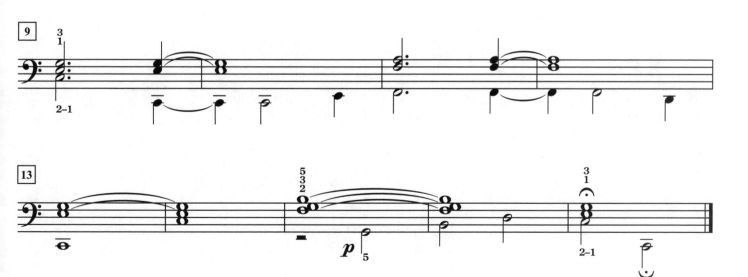

Don't Stop Believin'

Words and Music by Jonathan Cain,
Neal Schon and Steve Perry
Arranged by Carol Matz

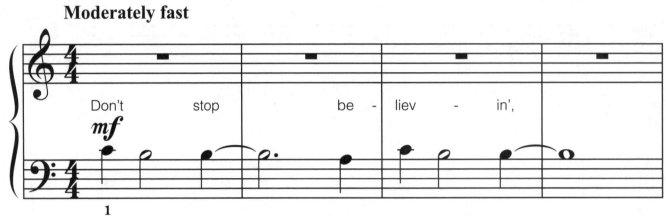

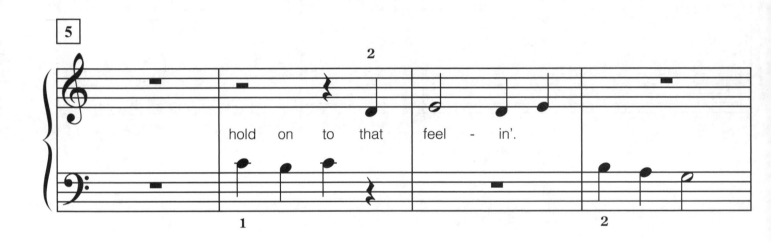

DUET PART (Student plays one octave higher)

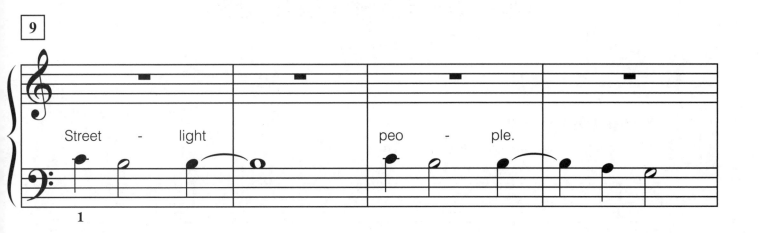

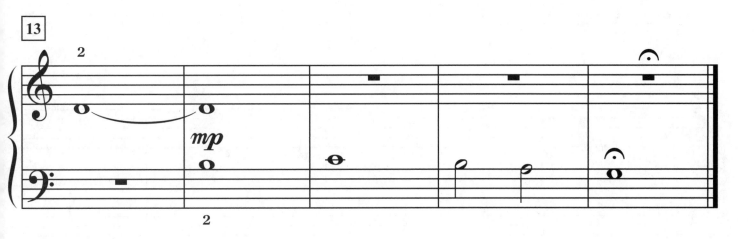

DUET PART (Continued)

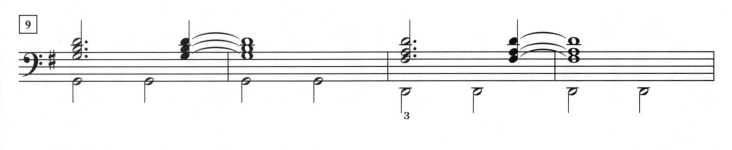

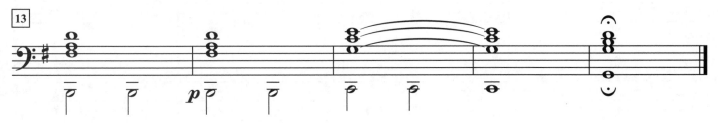

Camptown Races

Secondo

Stephen Foster
Arranged by Carol Matz

Moderately fast

Play both hands one octave lower

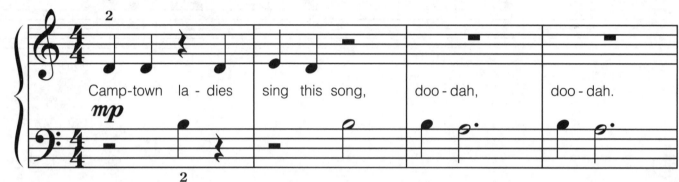

Camp-town la - dies sing this song, doo - dah, doo - dah.

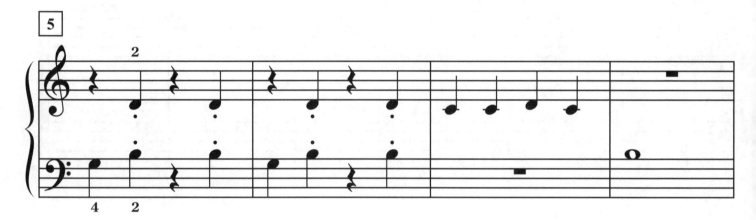

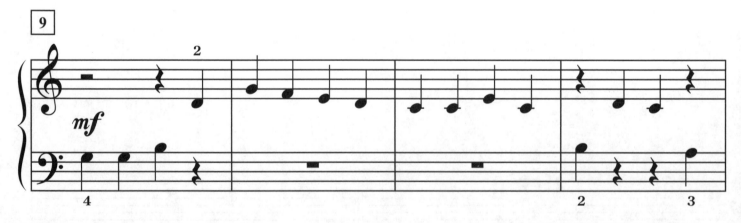

Camptown Races

Primo

Stephen Foster
Arranged by Carol Matz

Moderately fast

Play both hands one octave higher

Camp-town race-track five miles long, oh, de doo - dah day.

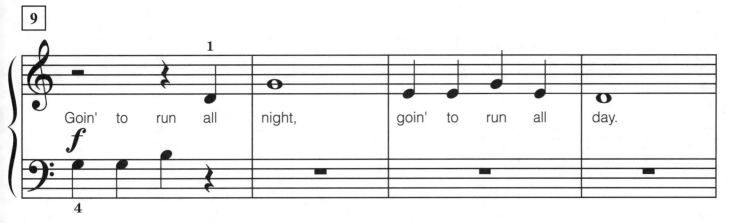

Goin' to run all night, goin' to run all day.

Bet my money on the bob - tail nag, some-body bet on the bay.

The Snake Charmer

Secondo

Traditional
Arranged by Carol Matz

Moderately fast
Play both hands one octave lower

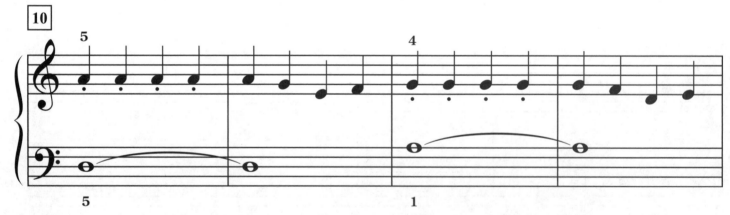

The Snake Charmer

Primo

Traditional
Arranged by Carol Matz

Moderately fast
Play both hands one octave higher

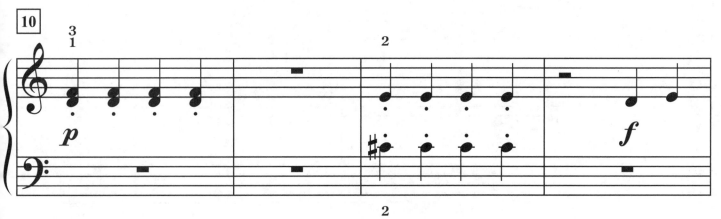

La Cucaracha

Secondo

Traditional
Arranged by Carol Matz

Moderately fast
Play both hands one octave lower

La Cucaracha

Primo

Traditional
Arranged by Carol Matz

Moderately fast

Play both hands one octave higher

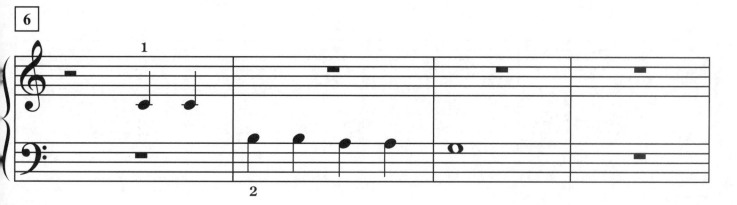

Yo Ho (A Pirate's Life for Me)

(from Walt Disney's "Pirates of the Caribbean")

Secondo

Words by Xavier Atencio
Music by George Bruns
Arranged by Carol Matz

With spirit

Play both hands one octave lower

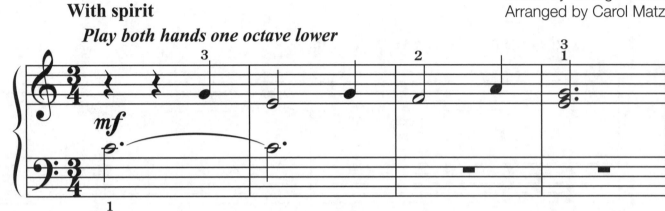

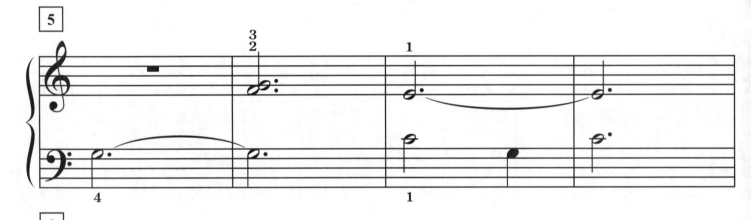

Yo Ho (A Pirate's Life for Me)

(from Walt Disney's "Pirates of the Caribbean")

Primo

Words by Xavier Atencio
Music by George Bruns
Arranged by Carol Matz

With spirit

Play both hands one octave higher

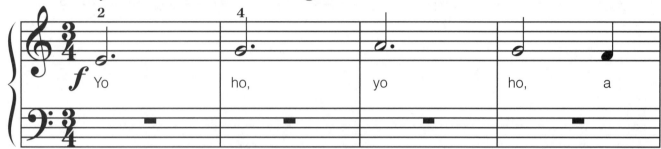

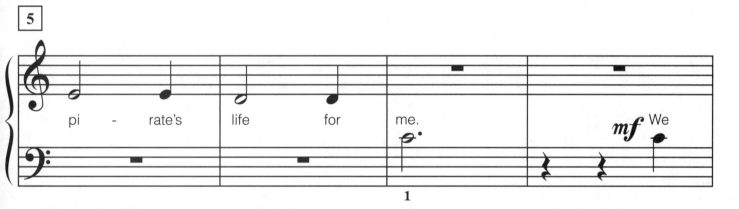

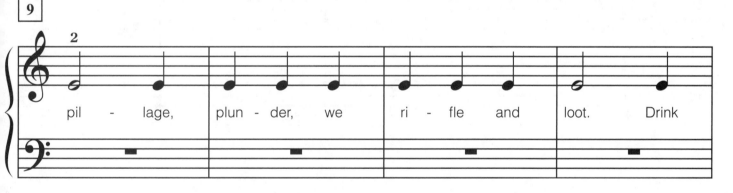

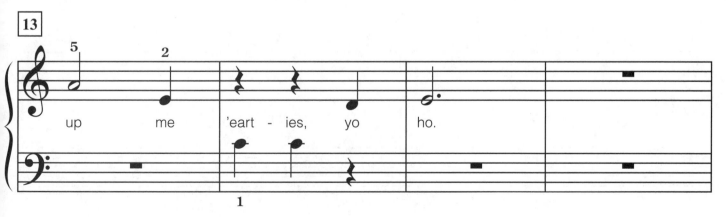

Secondo

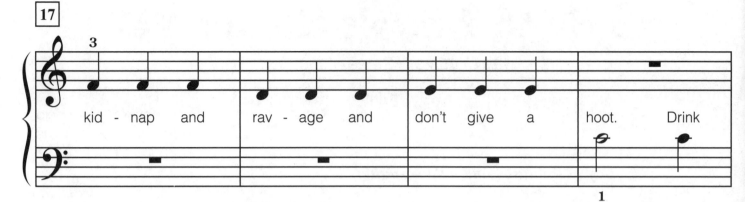

17 kid - nap and rav - age and don't give a hoot. Drink

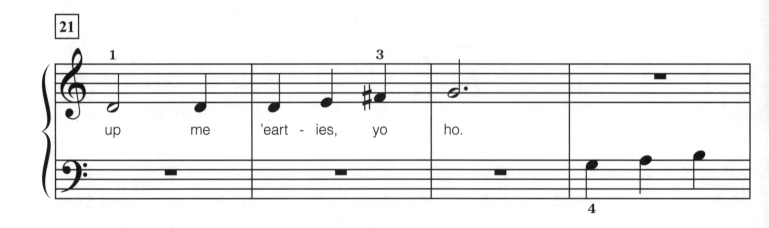

21 up me 'eart - ies, yo ho.

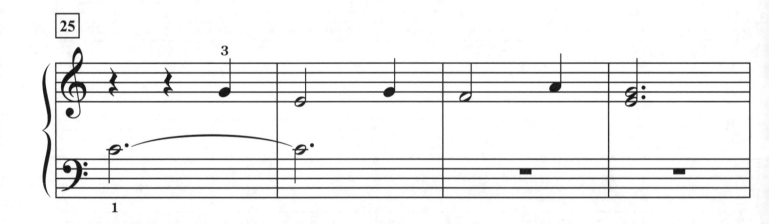

25

29

Primo

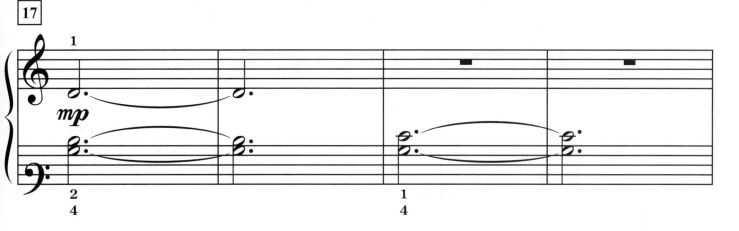

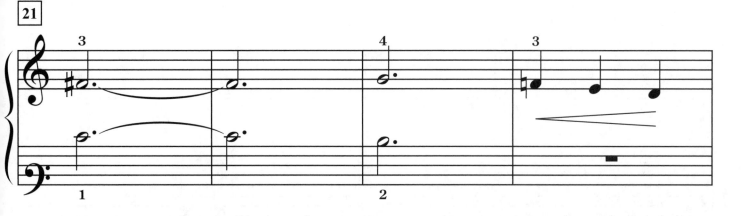

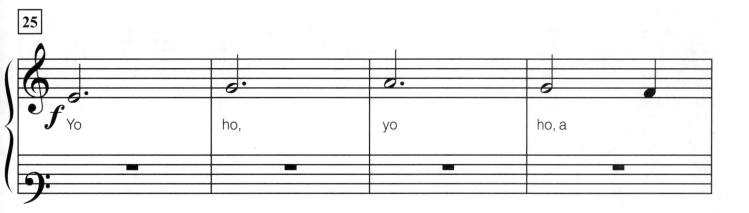

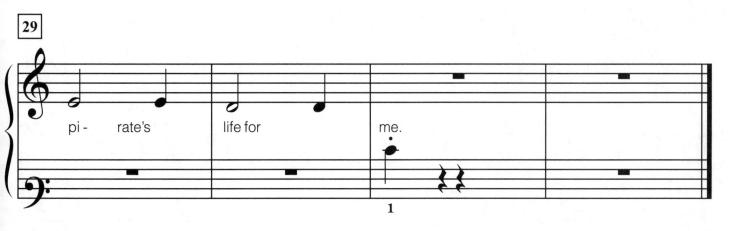

Itsy Bitsy Teenie Weenie Yellow Polka Dot Bikini

Secondo

Words and Music by
Paul J. Vance and Lee Pockriss
Arranged by Carol Matz

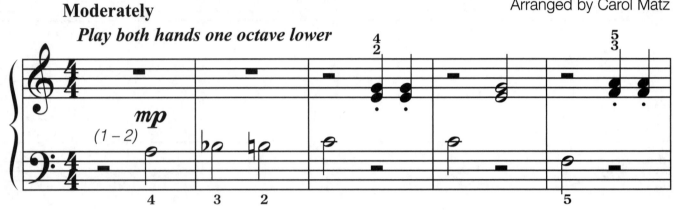

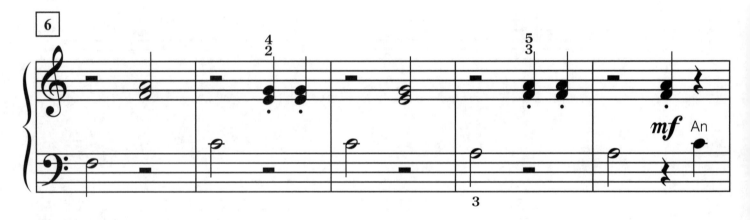

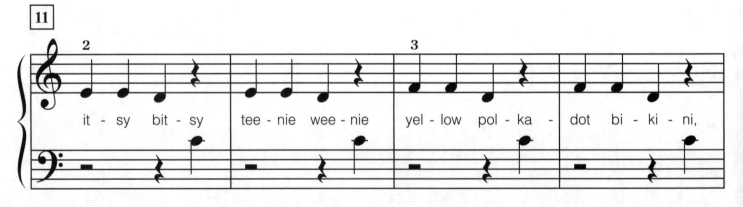

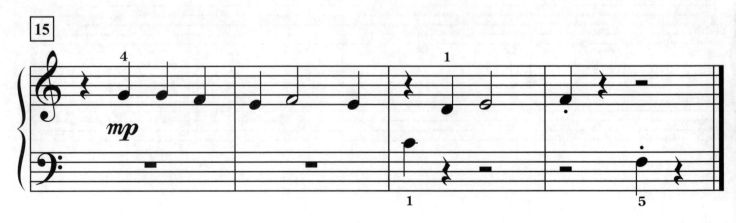

Itsy Bitsy Teenie Weenie Yellow Polka Dot Bikini

Primo

Words and Music by
Paul J. Vance and Lee Pockriss
Arranged by Carol Matz

Moderately
Play both hands one octave higher

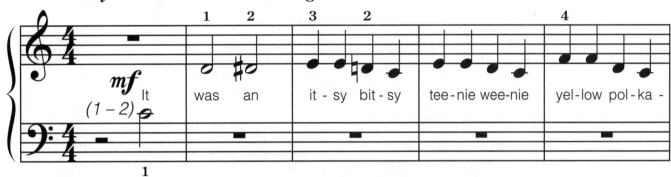

mf
(1 – 2)
It was an it-sy bit-sy tee-nie wee-nie yel-low pol-ka -

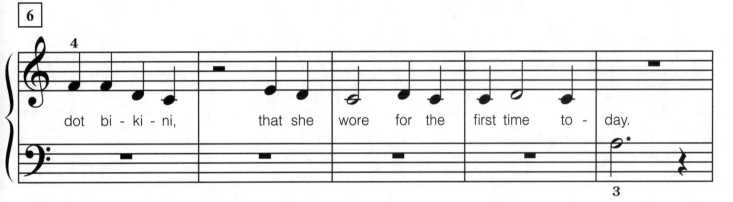

dot bi-ki-ni, that she wore for the first time to - day.

mp

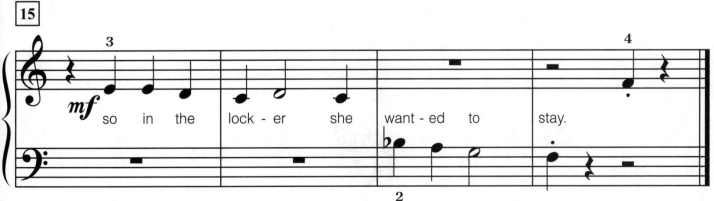

mf so in the lock-er she want-ed to stay.